AT HOME IN WORLD WAR TWO

RATIONING

Stewart Ross

Evans Brothers Limited

First published in paperback in 2007 by Evans Brothers Limited
2A Portman Mansions
Chiltern Street
London W1U 6NR

Produced for Evans Brothers Limited by
White-Thomson Publishing Ltd
210 High Street, Lewes,
East Sussex BN7 2NH

Printed in Dubai

Editor: Philippa Smith
Consultant: Terry Charman, Historian, Research and Information Department, Imperial War Museum
Designer: Christopher Halls, Mind's Eye Design, Lewes
Proofreader: Rosemary Ashley

British Library Cataloguing in Publication Data
Ross, Stewart
   Rationing. - (At home in World War Two)
   1. Rationing - Great Britain - History 2. World War, 1939-1945 - Food Supply - Great Britain 3. World War, 1939- 1945 - Social aspects - Great Britain
   I. Title
   941'.084
ISBN: 9780237533953

Captions:
Cover and this page: A Government poster encouraging people to recycle their waste food by giving it to farmers for pig food.
Cover (centre): A WVS (Women's Voluntary Service) mobile van brings hot meals to workers in the Kent countryside. As food was rationed during World War Two, any extra was very welcome.
Cover (background): Part of a typical emergency food store that a family of four was allowed to keep in 1942. Keeping more food than this was considered wasteful.
Title page: During the war everyone was issued with food and clothing ration books, like these.
Contents page: In 1940 the Government launched a 'Saucepans for Spitfires' appeal as aluminium was needed for making fighter aircraft. These schoolboys are displaying their collection of aluminium goods for recycling. The dogs have been put in the photograph for publicity – the gutsy bulldog was the symbol of Britain's determination to win the war.

For sources of quoted material see page 31.

CONTENTS

TOTAL WAR

Britain joined World War Two in September 1939 when it declared war on Germany. France, Belgium, the Netherlands, Poland and other countries fought with Britain against Germany and, later, against Italy. In 1941, the USSR and the USA joined the war on the same side as Britain. Japan joined the side of Germany and Italy. This spread the fighting right around the world. The war finally ended in 1945.

World War Two took place on land, at sea and in the air. Bombs dropped by enemy aircraft during air raids destroyed millions of homes and killed and injured many thousands of people. Everyone's home might be in the 'front line'. That is why we say the war was fought on the 'Home Front' as well as the battle front.

▶ *A newspaper seller carries
a poster telling passers-by of
the outbreak of war,
3 September 1939.*

World War Two was a 'total' war. This means that the warring countries did everything they could to win. Every person, every factory and every field was needed for the war effort. The manufacture of non-essential foods and goods, such as chocolate and fine clothes, was cut back and they became very difficult to obtain.

In 1939 two-thirds of Britain's food and many of industry's raw materials (oil and aluminium, for example) came from abroad. The enemy sank thousands of ships bringing these supplies to Britain, which led to severe shortages.

The Government coped with these problems in two ways. First, it encouraged more food and raw materials to be produced at home. Second, it cut back on the food and goods people could buy. The most important way of doing this was by rationing.

THE PATH TO WAR

Adolf Hitler became leader of Germany in 1933. Backed by his Nazi Party, he removed those who were against him and began taking over neighbouring countries. After Germany took over Czechoslovakia, Britain and France promised other countries that they would oppose Nazi aggression if the Germans attacked anyone else. On 1 September 1939, Hitler invaded Poland. Two days later, Britain and France declared war on Germany.

Luxuries were very difficult to obtain during the war. On 16 November 1940, the *Daily Herald* listed a whole range of items that its readers would probably have to do without:

'LUXURIES YOU MUST NOW DO WITHOUT
... include gloves, lace, furs, mattresses, corsets, carpets, linoleum, pottery, glass ... office furniture ... cutlery ... cameras, musical instruments, sports goods, toys, fancy goods, fountain pens, umbrellas ...'

◀ *The land you are fighting for ... This Government poster was not very realistic or popular – most Britons lived in towns and cities and rarely saw countryside like this.*

BATTLE OF THE ATLANTIC

In 1939 Britain had the largest merchant fleet in the world, more than the totals of the USA and Japan combined. In normal times this fleet had no trouble supplying the country with food and raw materials. But World War Two was not a normal time.

Between 1939 and 1945, 5,150 British ships were sunk by enemy action. The total tonnage lost was more than that of its entire pre-war fleet. Although new ships were built, bought or leased, and ships of other nations took over some of the trade, supplies were severely cut back.

The crisis was worst in the Atlantic, where shipping was attacked by German surface warships and submarines ('U-boats'). The situation was so serious by early 1941 that Prime Minister Winston Churchill called it the 'Battle of the Atlantic'. The following year, 1,006 merchant vessels were lost in the Atlantic.

SHE TALKED...

...THIS HAPPENED

CARELESS TALK COSTS LIVES

▲ The Government produced many posters warning the public that 'careless talk costs lives'. This poster shows a British ship that has been sunk, possibly because the enemy had discovered when and where the ship was sailing.

▶ An enemy bomb just misses a Royal Navy destroyer that is escorting British merchant ships on a dangerous convoy.

Joe Crooks, a young sailor aged 17:
'My last ship went down. Now I'm taking another. Got to. I'm broke.'

A mother who lost her husband in the Battle of the Atlantic remembered:
'When my first child was born my husband was at sea. When my second child was born he was dead.'

Ships travelled to and from Britain in 'convoys' – many vessels sailing together with an escort of destroyers and corvettes. A convoy, sailing at the speed of the slowest vessel, made a tempting target for a U-boat's torpedoes. The escorts had to locate a U-boat with underwater detection equipment ('sonar'), then attack it with depth charges (explosives that went off at a pre-set depth).

The tide of the battle finally turned in May 1943, when the Royal Navy sank 41 U-boats. From this time forward Britain's supplies were reasonably safe, although they did not return to normal until after the war.

THE
BRITISH NAVY
guards the freedom of us all

▲ A propaganda poster praising the Royal Navy. The ships, like the British people, are battling through difficult conditions towards their goal – victory.

◀ Part of a consignment of more than one million kilograms of New Zealand butter being unloaded in London docks.

7

A Fair Share for All

The Emergency Powers Acts of 1939 and 1940 gave the Government enormous power to direct the war effort. A Ministry of Labour and National Service organised what work people did and a Ministry of Food arranged for the country to be 'fed like an army.' Both were set up in 1939.

Cutting down on the amount of goods used was done in many different ways. High taxes, for instance, raised the price of products and so fewer were bought. In 1939 the tax on beer was £1.20 a barrel. By 1945 it had risen to £7.00 a barrel. Beer was also mixed with water to make it go further.

Products in short supply were substituted with others. Margarine was used instead of butter, for example, and powdered eggs for fresh eggs. Other well-known substitutes were various kinds of tinned and processed meats (such as 'Spam' – see page 12).

A popular wartime joke:
Barmaid, looking out of window after pouring a pint for a drinker:
'It looks like rain.'
Drinker, after taking a sip of his beer: 'Aye, and it tastes like it, too!'

How to reconstitute powdered egg:
To make one egg, mix one level tablespoonful of egg powder with two level tablespoonfuls of water. Allow to stand for about five minutes. Work out any lumps with a wooden spoon, finally beating with a fork or whisk. Use at once.

▶ *This woman has to buy processed pancake mixture. The packet on the counter contains powdered egg that, like the pancake mixture, had to be mixed with water.*

Scarce goods and luxuries like imported cars were either banned altogether or severely cut back. Petrol for private motorists was rationed until 1942, after which it was available only to essential users, such as doctors.

'It was announced last night that as from September 16 all petrol will be rationed. In the meantime all car owners are asked not to use their cars more than is vitally necessary.'

Daily Mirror, 4 September 1939

Butter, bacon and sugar were rationed from January 1940. Rationing was soon extended to other foods and goods and, in 1941, to clothes. This had a double purpose. It limited the amount of food or goods bought and made sure they were distributed fairly. Everyone, rich and poor, was given coupons for all rationed goods. These had to be handed over when buying something 'on rations'.

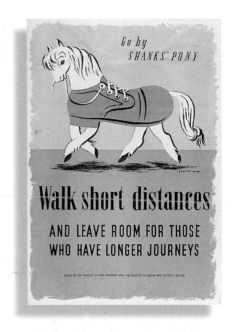

▲ A Government poster urging people to save petrol by travelling on foot – 'Shanks' pony'. Walking was also good exercise. During the war people ate less and took more exercise, and the nation's health improved.

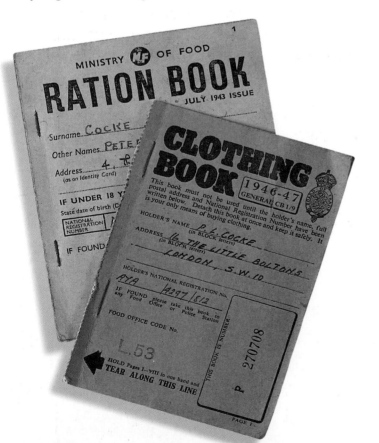

▲ Food and clothing ration books. It was illegal to use someone else's ration book. Food was rationed until 1954, clothing until 1949.

'For wasting petrol by leaving his lorry engine running for two minutes, Thomas Waters of Bridge Street, Whitney, was yesterday fined 5 shillings [25p].'

Daily Express, 18 October 1941

'Owing to rationing and Government orders we have been unable to supply our customers in full. We regret the disappointment this has caused.'

Notice added to advertisements for Cadbury's chocolate, 1940

CUTTING THE COUPONS

In pre-war Britain most food and goods were bought from small specialist shops. During the war, as this woman from the East End of London remembers, customers had to decide where they wanted to do their shopping – and stick to their choices:

> 'We had to choose particular shops – butcher, grocer, dairy – to go to, then you always had to take your ration book there, because you were registered there, and couldn't shop for rationed goods anywhere else. Shopkeepers then got supplies according to the number of registered customers they had. They always had a few stores to cope with emergencies too.'

Food rationing began on 8 January 1940. Coupons for rationed foods were contained in ration books which could be collected from Ministry of Food offices situated in towns up and down the country.

Shoppers had to register with local shopkeepers. When they bought 'on ration' food the shopkeeper cut the coupon for that food from the book. The coupons had to be used before they expired: if you did not use your 2 oz (50 g) tea ration one week, for example, you were not allowed to buy 4 oz (100 g) the next week.

As ordinary tea was rationed, this alternative was suggested:

NETTLE TEA

Gather young stinging nettles. Remember to put on an old pair of gloves for picking. Wash and dry the nettles in the sun. When dry, crumble up and boil in water to draw out the flavour. Nettle tea once a day makes a good, healthy drink.

▶ *No exceptions – the ration book of Princess Elizabeth, now Queen Elizabeth II. The Princess had a special 'Traveller's Ration Book', issued to people who could not always shop in the same place.*

Shopkeepers and shoppers caught cheating were severely punished, and the system worked quite well. The amount of butter and margarine bought, for example, was halved. But there were problems. Until it was rationed in 1941, cheese was scarce, and the summer of 1940 saw a severe 'egg famine'.

Some examples of rations per person:
(N.B. amounts changed according to the season and supplies available)

1940 butter 4 oz [100 g] per week (2 oz [50 g] in 1943)
1940 4 oz [100 g] bacon/ham per week
1940 sugar 12 oz [300 g] per week (8 oz [200 g] in 1942)
1940 tea 2 oz [50 g] per week
1941 cheese 1 oz [25 g] per week
1941 soap 1 lb [450 g] for 4 weeks
1943 cooking fat 2 oz [50 g] per week
1943 margarine 4 oz [100 g] per week (with added vitamins)
1943 eggs 4 per month

Beef and lamb were rationed by cost. In 1940 the allowance was one shilling and ten pence [9 p]; by 1943 it had fallen to one shilling and tuppence [6 p].

▼ *A Londoner making breakfast using some of his 4 oz (100 g) weekly bacon ration and one of his four eggs per month.*

'Sugar Coupon No. 6 is available this week, for an extra 2 lbs [1 kg] of sugar for jam-making. Ask your grocer for yours straight away.'

Daily Express,
14 August 1940

◄ *Doing their bit for the war. Members of a Women's Institute in south-east England making jam. Their efforts meant that wild fruits, such as blackberries, were not wasted.*

SPAM

From December 1941 certain foods could be bought with 'points'. Each person had 16 points a month (later raised to 20) with which to buy things like tinned fish. A tin of Spam (spiced ham) used up 16 points. A large bag of dried peas or three-quarters of a tin of salmon used up 20 points.

The British became used to Spam and other tinned meat products like 'Mor'. Common long-lasting foods included powdered eggs, evaporated milk, and tinned bacon and ham. America supplied 7 per cent of Britain's food as part of the Lend-Lease scheme (1941) by which supplies did not have to be paid for immediately.

▲ Spam – spiced ham – was imported from America to make up for the shortage of home-produced meat. Most people got used to the taste. The same could not be said of another wartime import, whale meat, which was unpleasantly oily.

▶ Boys tuck into eggs sent from America. The 'Uncle Sam' figure on the board behind them represents the USA.

Wartime production of pig meat fell by two-thirds and egg output halved. Biscuits, sweets and even milk were rationed. Oranges and bananas were very rare luxuries. These wartime shortages changed eating habits and forced cooks to become more inventive and imaginative. The BBC's Radio Doctor and the Ministry of Food Research Kitchen gave advice for using home-grown food: the belief that carrots help you to see in the dark, for example, started as wartime propaganda.

Interestingly, people's diet was generally healthier than before the war. This was partly because less meat, sugar and fat was eaten. Also, it was common for both parents to work, so there were fewer very poor families. Rationing and Government schemes to supply milk and vitamins ensured that everyone, especially poor children, received their fair share of what was available.

▲ As bananas were almost unobtainable during the war, a whole generation of children grew up not knowing what they were. When they were first given bananas after the war, some children saved the skins for re-filling!

ENGLISH MONKEY (economical scrambled eggs)

1 reconstituted egg (see page 8)
1 cup stale breadcrumbs
1 cup milk
½ cup grated cheese
1 tablespoon margarine
½ teaspoon salt
Pepper

Method: Soak the breadcrumbs in the milk. Melt the margarine in a pan and add the cheese. When melted add the soaked breadcrumbs, egg (well beaten), salt and pepper. Cook for three minutes. Spread on toast.

◄ The Government started the 'Doctor Carrot' campaign to get children to eat more carrots, which were not rationed. They were a good source of vitamin A. 'Potato Pete' (who had his own song) was another cartoon character used to persuade people to eat cheap, home-grown food. Recipes even appeared for potato cakes and potato sandwiches! The more potatoes were eaten, the less wheat had to be imported from abroad to make bread.

THE BLACK MARKET

Wartime shopping was a dreary business – returning to the same shops every time and often standing in long queues for bread, potatoes, green vegetables, fruit and fish. It was not just goods that were in short supply, either. In some towns 20 per cent of shops closed down, giving customers even less choice.

► *Shoppers standing in a queue at a grocer's shop. People got used to queuing for almost everything. Because shops soon ran out of popular goods, a well-known wartime saying was, 'If you see a queue, join it!'*

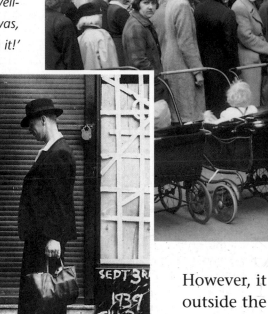

▲ *The owner of this boarded-up shoe repair shop tells his customers that he has been 'called up' into the armed forces. He says he'll be back when Hitler has been defeated – in other words, when the war is over. (O.H.M.S. stands for On His Majesty's Service.)*

However, it was possible to buy goods illegally outside the rationing and points systems. This was called the 'black market'. Marjorie Bliss, who worked as a physiotherapist in Stoke Mandeville Hospital near Aylesbury, remembers: '*We often bought up other people's coupons. If someone didn't like butter, I got hold of their ration straight away. Shopkeepers just turned a blind eye.*

But that wasn't really the black market – that was getting hold of things you weren't meant to. It was always possible because there were shady-looking men in raincoats who could find anything. When I was seriously ill in hospital my brother-in-law got an orange for me. I don't know where from. I was given all sorts of things by private patients. They paid me things like eggs or clothes. No one asked where they came from.'

Although the black market was illegal, many people used it. For example, Land Army women (see page 22) needed their clothing points to obtain their uniforms. If they wanted new civilian clothes they had either to make them or buy them on the black market. Black market salesmen made huge profits: sugar sold at three times its normal price and a cigar worth 2.5p fetched 25p.

▶ *Land Army girls protesting that their clothing ration and pay was far less than that of the ATS (Auxiliary Territorial Service, the women's branch of the army).*

Selling goods on the black market was punishable by heavy fines or even imprisonment:
'*After passing sentence in a black market case at Manchester Assizes yesterday, Mr Justice Wrottesley made an order for the goods concerned to be handed over to the Board of Trade and disposed of "for the good of the country".*'

News Chronicle, 7 December 1943

▶ *A soldier guards goods salvaged from a grocer's bombed shop after an air raid on Liverpool, March 1941. If the soldier hadn't been there, the goods might well have been stolen and sold on the black market.*

EATING OUT

Food in restaurants was unrationed, although supplies were limited according to the number of customers. There were no 'fast-food' restaurants in Britain then, and normally only middle- and upper-class people went out for restaurant meals. Consequently, the decision not to ration restaurants was said to favour the well-off. In 1942 the Government responded by limiting the price of meals to five shillings [25p], with only one main course per person.

The Government banned ice cream as an unnecessary luxury. Ice cream makers were not pleased, as you can tell from this article in the *Daily Express*, 26 June 1942:

> 'The Ice Cream Association's Joint War Emergency Committee, which says it was not consulted by the Ministry of Food, is to negotiate with the Ministry about the ban on the making of ice cream from September 30.'

▲ A waitress waters tomatoes and lettuces planted in boxes outside a smart restaurant in London's West End, 1940.

> 'Victory dishes, marked "V" on the menu, will soon be available in restaurants.'

Daily Telegraph, 27 January 1943

'Victory' meals consisted of ingredients that were not in short supply.

The wartime demand for aircraft, tanks, munitions and other armaments was enormous. New factories were built and old ones converted to make war supplies. To meet the demand for labour, everyone under the age of 51 was registered for war work.

► What a laugh! Well-fed munition factory workers enjoy a break from their work. Their caps and thick overalls are to protect them from dangerous chemicals.

Many men and women worked a 60-hour week, leaving little time for shopping. So that they could get at least one good meal a day, the Government encouraged factories to set up their own canteens. These always received plentiful food supplies. The school meal service expanded, too.

The Government also established over 2,000 'British Restaurants', situated in almost any suitable space, from parish halls to museum galleries. By 1943 they were serving 700,000 meals a day. A main dish cost 8 pence [about 3p], pudding 4 pence [less than 2p] and a cup of tea tuppence [less than 1p]. A full meal cost 1 shilling and tuppence [about 6p]. These measures led to the number of meals eaten outside the home rising from 79 million in 1941 to 170 million in 1944.

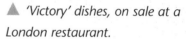

▲ 'Victory' dishes, on sale at a London restaurant.

◀ Men and women enjoying a meal in a British Restaurant. No one has taken their coat off because, to save fuel, there was little heating in public places during the war.

HARD TIMES

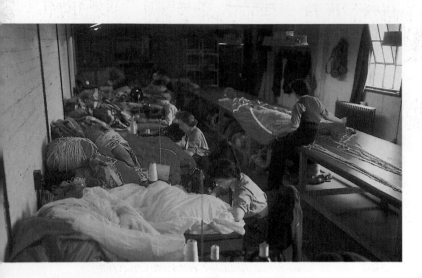

▲ Women making parachutes, May 1944. During the war many clothing factories changed to making uniforms and equipment needed by the armed forces.

In 1939–41 the cost of raw materials, such as metals, rubber, wood and cotton, more than doubled. War needs were given priority over civilian needs. Clothing factories, for example, switched to making uniforms and parachutes. As fewer civilian goods were manufactured, there were shortages of everyday household articles like cooking utensils, furniture and clothes.

The Government tackled the problem in three ways. First, on 1 June 1941, clothes rationing began. For a while there were no separate clothes coupons, so food coupons had to be used. Clothes were rationed by 'points': 66 points per person per year (reduced to 48 points in 1942). In 1943 a special child clothes ration was introduced. Its formula of birthday, height and weight was too complicated for many families to understand.

Clothing rations in the first year of the war (assuming the clothes could be found in the shops):

Men: 1 pair of boots or shoes; 6 pairs of socks; 1 suit (without a waistcoat); 1 overcoat; a few detachable collars, handkerchiefs and ties.

Women: 1 pair of shoes; 6 pairs of stockings; 10 oz (250 g) of wool or 2.5 yards [2.3 m] of material, 1 suit, 1 overcoat, 2 slips, 1 blouse.

Note: the lists are more interesting for what they leave out rather than what they contain. Which garments are missing?

▲ A little girl, who has lost all her clothes in a bombing raid, tries on a new pullover sent from America.

Second, in 1941, 'utility' clothes and other goods were introduced. Designed by fashion experts, the clothes were simple, cheap and quite stylish. In 1943 a utility dress used 11 points and a pair of utility knickers two points. By the end of the war about 80 per cent of all new clothes were utility designed. The Prime Minister, Winston Churchill, set an example by appearing in public wearing a one-piece utility boiler suit, known as a 'siren suit'.

Third, the 1942 austerity regulations (a Government scheme to save labour and materials), cut back the amount of cloth and labour used in non-utility clothes. They limited the number of seams, pleats, button holes and pockets, banned turn-ups and even set maximum lengths for socks at 9.5 inches [24 cm].

▲ Prime Minister Winston Churchill insisted on wearing his wartime boiler suit (known as a 'siren suit') even when visiting the President of the United States. He is shown here on the lawn of the President's official residence, the White House.

Because clothes were so scarce, Mrs Ellen Knight of the Wirral, Cheshire, and her friends used to wear their working clothes to dances:

'We had very few civvy [civilian] clothes as we had to use our clothing coupons for our Land Army uniforms etc., so with our clean pressed dungarees, we hit the dance floor.'

◄ The height of fashion? A girl models a green 'austerity' dress and jacket. The objects in the sky are barrage balloons, flown as part of the country's defences against low-flying aircraft.

MAKING DO

MENDING LACE OR NET CURTAINS

It's a simple matter if you have a piece of similar material large enough to extend well over the torn part. Put the curtain flat on a table with an ironing blanket under the place to be repaired. Dip the patch into rice-water, wring out well, spread it over the hole and press with a hot iron.

▲ ▶ *Government tips on how children can help with home repairs. They were presented as separate tips for boys and girls, which nowadays would be considered sexist.*

How to Refix LOOSE CASTERS

Shaky casters on chair or table legs are usually due to loose screws. The cup caster type should be taken off and re-placed so that the screws will go into new holes. (The old holes can be filled up with plastic wood). To deal with a pin caster —the kind which has a single screw that goes in the centre of the leg —take the caster off and fill in the screw hole with a mix-ture of sawdust and glue. Allow this to harden and then replace the caster.

One of the Government's most powerful campaigns was 'Make-do and Mend'. As Lavinia Gerrard, who worked as a secretary in London, remembered, it made everyone a do-it-yourself expert:

'I think the war made us careful for the rest of our lives. You see, we were always being told not to waste anything, to mend things, to use substitutes. Even now, when I throw away an empty biro, I feel a bit guilty because it hasn't been refilled. In the war there was no such thing as "it's easier to get a new one."

I went to a friend's wedding, in 1943 I think it was. Everything was second-hand; she even wore her mother's wedding dress. A friend made the cake out of whatever she could get hold of, like hazel-nuts and margarine. There was only a thin bit of icing on the top. I can't remember what we drank the toast in, but it wasn't champagne. Probably cider.'

Newspapers offered useful making-do tips for things like dyeing clothes, re-heeling shoes and making tasty meals from off-ration food, such as offal. Women painted their legs to look like stockings. Some dogs and cats were even combed for 'wool'.

◀ *Schoolboys from London, evacuated to Devon, learning how to mend boots and shoes. New shoes were expensive and used up many coupons, so it was essential to keep old pairs going for as long as possible.*

The Government encouraged and regulated at every stage. It offered make-do suggestions from 'Mrs Sew-and-Sew'. 'Squanderbug' posters encouraged people not to waste anything. But when women began making curtains into clothes, the practice was banned: curtains were needed to 'black out' houses at night so that enemy bombers could not see the lights.

'Now when you must economise a Singer Sewing Machine can save you pounds. You can make all your own garments and household requirements.'

Advertisement for Singer sewing machines, 1940

▲ *Mrs Sew-and-Sew (yet another of the Government's cartoon figures) tells mothers how to shop wisely for children's underclothes. After a while, bossy instructions like these began to annoy people.*

'Are you coupon starved? Give your new but faded clothes new life with Tintex. This wonderful home dye does the most amazing things with old and faded garments. Newer, prettier undies!'

An advertisement, 1943

◄ *Make-do and Mend. A Government announcement shows how a woman cut up two old dresses to make one 'new' one. She saved seven coupons by making her own dress – and another two by turning left-over material into a pair of knickers!*

IN THE FIELDS

▼ A Government poster encouraging women to help with farmwork.

Come and help with the VICTORY HARVEST

You are needed in the fields!

APPLY TO NEAREST EMPLOYMENT EXCHANGE FOR LEAFLET & ENROLMENT FORM OR WRITE DIRECT TO THE DEPARTMENT OF AGRICULTURE FOR SCOTLAND 15 GROSVENOR STREET, EDINBURGH.

In 1940 Dora Ellis, a Birmingham girl, joined the Women's Land Army and was sent to help on a farm near Norwich:

'I'd never seen a real cow until now, and what a shock it all was to me . . . I was scared stiff of them, and stood there in fear when a voice bellowed out, "Well, don't jist look at 'em, girl – git milking 'em." I didn't know where to start . . . Should I pump the tail to get the milk out or what? . . . The dairyman could see this and came over to me and said, "All right, don't get upset, me love. I can show you what to do." It was horrible, for just as I did start to get the hang of it, the cow went and kicked the bucket of milk all over me. I was crying and feeling very upset, and wanted my mum!'

Dora was one of 80,000 young Land Army women. They replaced male agricultural workers who had joined the armed forces, and worked tirelessly to increase the output from Britain's farms.

▼ Members of the Women's Land Army collecting sheaves of corn at harvest time. There was far less farm machinery than today, and much of the work had to be done by hand.

◄ *Not quite what I was trained to do . . . The Land Army woman driving this caterpillar tractor was a dressmaker before the war.*

During the war 2.5 million more hectares of land were ploughed up. The number of tractors (often driven by women) rose from 56,000 to 545,000. Combine harvesters and other machines were introduced and inefficient farmers were forced to hand over their farms to others. As a result, the proportion of Britain's food that came from abroad fell from two-thirds in 1939 to one-third by 1945.

Speaking in Parliament, Lord Woolton, Minister of Food, had great praise for British farmers:

> 'We tell them what we want. We pitch our requirements high. We ask what would not long ago have been thought unattainable. They do not flinch. They set about meeting the demands.'
Scottish Daily Express, 14 May 1943

'I wanted to do something that I thought I would like to do instead of having to do what I was told to do, so that's why I chose the Land Army.'

Dorothy Barton

► *Women volunteers harvesting cattle food. They are working by moonlight in an effort to get the crop in on time. Such remarkable dedication was quite common in wartime.*

DIG FOR VICTORY!

Food was not only produced on farms but in all kinds of unusual places. All over the country public parks and commons, private lawns, city gardens and even railway embankments were dug up and planted with corn, vegetables, potatoes and other crops.

It was estimated that by 1943 2.5 million gardens were producing food worth about £12 million a year. The rolling grassland of Windsor Great Park, owned by the Royal Family, was turned into the largest cornfield in the country. Urged on by the Government's 'Dig for Victory' campaign, 750,000 allotment owners (or, more usually, their wives) also did their bit to boost the supply of home-grown food.

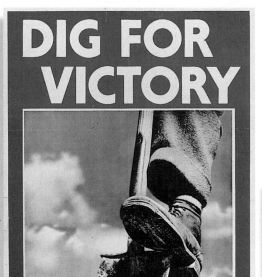

In 1940 *Vogue* magazine urged its readers to play their part in feeding the nation:
'Now is the time to plough up the park and make over flower beds for vegetables.'

▲ An office worker uses his lunch hour to hoe onions planted on the roof of a London office block. St Paul's Cathedral can be seen in the background.

▲ ▶ The Government began its 'Dig for Victory' campaign in 1940. It encouraged people to plant crops and vegetables in every spare piece of soil they could find – even in window boxes.

To help out with the shortage of farm labour, 200,000 townspeople went to work on farms during their holidays. Back home, people living in streets and blocks of flats clubbed together to buy chickens and pigs which were kept in back gardens and on waste ground. A new phrase entered the language: 'Tottenham Cake', meaning the scraps dustmen saved from waste bins to feed their pigs.

Women's Institutes, working voluntarily, played an important part in food production, too. By the end of 1941 they were making 4,500 tonnes of jam and 120 tonnes of bottled fruit a year. They also rediscovered the value of natural medicines and tonics. In one year, for example, they picked 134 million wild rose hips that were made into a vitamin-rich syrup for children.

'One way to guard against invasion is to plough up and plant each expanse of flat ground.'

'York council estate tenants, who were once forbidden to keep poultry in their gardens, must now dig for victory or get out.'

Daily Express, 31 May 1940

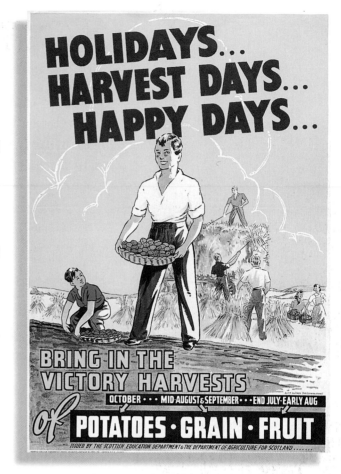

▲ Holiday jobs. This Scottish poster asked young people to spend their holidays helping with the harvest. Schools also dug up their playing fields and planted them with vegetables.

◀ Best use for a bomb site. Boys from Bethnal Green, London, clearing a patch of land on which houses had once stood. They are preparing the ground as a vegetable patch.

SALVAGE

In 1940 the 'Great Saucepan Offensive' began. Its aim was to get the public to donate recyclable metal, particularly aluminium pots and pans, for aircraft manufacture. The campaign was remarkably successful: thousands of tonnes of scrap were collected, including a complete set of kitchenware from the Royal Family and 500 tonnes of pans from the War Office.

'Very few of us can be heroines on the battle front, but we can all have the tiny thrill of thinking as we hear the news of an epic battle in the air, "Perhaps it was my saucepan that made part of that Hurricane".'

Lady Reading, the head of the WVS, in June 1940

▲ A 'Salvage Day' in London's Trafalgar Square. The message at the foot of Nelson's column is based on Nelson's famous message, 'England expects every man will do his duty.' In World War Two, however, salvage was done largely by women.

The public was asked, and sometimes told, to surrender all other unwanted metal objects, even thimbles. Twenty-four old keys, they were told, made a hand grenade, and 42 made a steel helmet. Householders volunteered miles of iron railings. When some remained standing, in September 1941 the Government ordered that those not needed for safety reasons must be handed over for scrap.

▶ A young boy carries an aluminium bath to the recycling centre. In the 1940s many city homes had no bathrooms, so metal baths like the one in the picture were very common.

Salvage – collecting material for recycling – became a national obsession. Bins were placed on street corners for bones, wool and paper. The Women's Voluntary Service (WVS) provided Salvage Wardens and Savings Collectors (wearing a brown badge with an 'S' on it), some of whom travelled round with the dustmen making sure that nothing useful was thrown away.

By 1943 half the country's paper was being recycled. Fifty million unwanted books (some of them rather valuable) were handed in and pulped. Children who helped in this campaign were rewarded with badges and army-style ranks. A child who brought in a few books became a 'private' and was allowed to wear a white badge, while one who appeared with dozens of volumes was made a 'general'.

PLACE YOUR FOOD WASTE HERE

EVERY OUNCE COUNTS

▲ Hope the pigs like it! Two housewives put their kitchen scraps into the 'pig bin'. The Government was very keen on catchy slogans like 'Every Ounce [25 g] Counts'.

◀ Boy Scouts, Cubs and Sea Scouts in Balderton, Nottinghamshire, load their collections of waste paper onto a salvage cart. Owing to the shortage of fuel, horses were widely used for pulling carts like these.

A HEALTHIER NATION

The most obvious result of the wartime measures to save food, materials and labour, some of which lasted until 1954, was that they did what they set out to do. Britain used its labour and resources more efficiently than any other country involved in the war. Other results were perhaps more surprising.

Overall, the health of the nation improved. Children in particular benefited, especially those from poorer homes. More school meals, the National Milk Scheme and the provision of free cod liver oil and orange juice meant children were better nourished than before the war. Adult health was helped by adequate meals in workplaces and British Restaurants. High prices, rationing and irregular supplies reduced people's intake of alcohol, tobacco and fats.

▲ Peace – but still no bread. This bread queue in Bermondsey, London, was photographed after the end of the war in Europe. The rationing of some goods, such as meat, continued for another nine years, until 1954.

'Britons are healthier today! Children are taller and stronger.'

From an advertisement for Allinson Bread and Flour, 1943

▶ Leaner and fitter. Despite the food shortages, the Government made a huge effort to see that children were well nourished. As a result of measures such as free cod liver oil and orange juice, which supplied extra vitamins, young children grew up fitter than they had been before the war.

mother

don't forget baby's

COD LIVER OIL
AND ORANGE JUICE

The war was marked by a strong community spirit: the nation survived only by everyone working together. Government measures played a part in building this mood of co-operation. Rationing, like enemy bombs, did not distinguish between rich and poor, men and women. Pre-war Britain had been strongly divided between the upper, middle and working classes. The war did not end these divisions, but it did help to weaken them.

'There was friendliness, kindness in the war. People forgot their pettinesses. They shared. If you had a car (I'd got rid of mine) you could pick up anyone and safely give them a lift. Somehow the war brought out the good in us.'

May Lawton, a teacher who worked as an ambulance driver

The wartime Government took a tighter control than ever before over industry and individual lives. This paved the way for a full 'welfare state'. With measures such as the Family Allowance Act (1945) and the National Health Act (1946), the post-war Labour Government undertook to care for people 'from the cradle to the grave'.

▲ *We've done our bit! Citizens of Belfast, Northern Ireland, proudly display the mountain of scrap iron they have collected. The flags and messages illustrate their vigorous community spirit.*

◀ *A decent meal at last. The Williams family get together in May 1945 to celebrate the end of the war.*

GLOSSARY

Act A law.

armaments Weapons of war.

armed forces The army, navy and air force.

Blitz The heavy bombing of a city. 'Blitz' comes from the German word *Blitzkrieg* which means 'lightning war'.

British Restaurants Restaurants set up by the Government to provide cheap, healthy meals.

called up Required to join the armed forces or do other war work.

canteen A place where food and drink is served.

civilian Someone not in the armed forces.

evacuate To move people to a safer place.

famine A severe shortage, usually of food.

illegal Against the law.

import To bring in goods from other countries.

invade To move into another country by force. In 1940 the Germans invaded France and planned to invade Britain.

lease An agreement to lend something.

Lend-Lease scheme An American agreement (1941) to provide Britain (and other countries) with war supplies. In return, the Americans used British military bases.

merchant fleet A country's cargo-carrying ships.

ministry A Government department, e.g. the Ministry of Food.

munitions Weapons and ammunition.

Nazi Party Germany's National Socialist Party. It was led by Adolf Hitler and followed his ideas and wishes.

negotiate To discuss a problem in order to reach an agreement.

offal The internal parts of an animal not normally eaten, such as the heart and brains.

offensive A large-scale attack.

post-war After the war.

processed Manufactured or altered in a factory.

propaganda Information that tries to raise people's spirits, or lower the spirits of the enemy.

rationing Limiting the amount of food and other goods people could buy and sharing it out equally.

reconstitute To restore a food (e.g. an egg) to its natural state by adding water.

salvage To collect material for recycling.

squander To waste.

tax Money collected by the Government to run the country.

tenant Someone who rents their home from someone else.

utility Low-cost clothing and other goods.

voluntary Something one can choose to do – or not.

War Office The Government department responsible for running the war.

Women's Institute A women's voluntary organisation set up to help the community.

Women's Land Army This was formed in June 1939. It recruited women to work in the countryside on farms, as Britain needed as much home-produced food as possible.

WVS The Women's Voluntary Service, which organised a range of wartime services, from mobile canteens to collecting scrap metal.

PROJECTS ON RATIONING

Write down everything you eat and drink in a day. Write out the list again, leaving out everything that would not have been available during World War Two.

Plan two days' wartime menu for a family of four. Which items could you grow in your garden or allotment?

A project on wartime rationing needs information from *primary* and *secondary* sources. Secondary sources, mainly books and websites, are listed on the next page. They give mostly other people's views about rationing. Primary sources come from the time of war itself, like some of the quotations in this book. They make a project really interesting and original.

Here are some ways to find primary information:
- Talking to people who lived through the war.
- Looking for objects remaining from the time of rationing. These might be ration books, newspapers or even utility clothes or books produced under austerity regulations.
- Visiting museums. Most local museums have excellent displays about their area during World War Two. National museums, like the Imperial War Museum in London, are packed with fascinating information.
- Reading printed memories. Your local library will probably have collections made from your local area.
- Visiting websites that contain primary information – but read the warning on the next page first!

FURTHER INFORMATION

BOOKS TO READ

Britain Through the Ages: Britain Since 1930, Stewart Ross (Evans, 1995)
Family Life: Second World War, Nigel Smith (Hodder Wayland, 1998)
The History Detective Investigates Britain at War: Rationing, Martin Parsons (Hodder Wayland, 2000)
Documenting the Past: The Second World War, Christine Hatt (Evans, 2007)
Family Scrapbook: A Wartime Childhood, Rebecca Hunter (Evans, 2005)
Investigating the Home Front, Alison Honey (The National Trust, 1996)
Memories of Childhood (The classic stories of **War Boy** and **After the War Was Over**), Michael Foreman (Pavilion, 2000)

WEBSITES

Just because information is on the web, it does not mean it is true. Well-known organisations like the BBC, a university or the Imperial War Museum, have sites you can trust. If you are unsure about a site, ask your teacher. Here are a few useful sites to start from (don't forget http:// or http://www.):

angelfire.com/la/raeder/England.html
bbc.co.uk/ww2peopleswar
bbc.co.uk/history/ww2children/ration/ration_intro.shtml
edencamp.co.uk/hut3/index.htm
historyplace.com/worldwar2
iwm.org.uk/lambeth/lambeth.htm

Picture acknowledgements:
The following images courtesy of the Imperial War Museum. Figures following page numbers refer to photograph negative numbers: Cover and imprint page poster: PST0705, cover (centre): HU63738, cover (background): V110, title page: IWM 01/02/1, contents page: HU36208, p.4: HU36171, p.5: PST2802, p.6 (top): Art Dept poster *She talked ... this happened,* (bottom): A12022, p.7 (top): PS0024, (bottom): D509, p.8: D2374, p.9 (top): 3121, (bottom): IWM01/02/1, p.10: D420, p.11 (top): D265, (bottom): D4857, p.12 (bottom): HU63768, p.13 (top): HU63736, (centre left): 6080, (centre right): PST8105, p.14 (right): D25035, (left): SG12898, p.15 (top): HU63784, (bottom): H8143, p.16 (top left): HU63825, (bottom): D671, p.17 (top): Victory dishes, (bottom): D12268, p.18 (top): TR1783, (bottom): D2088, p.19 (top): A6919, (bottom): D14817, p.20: (bottom): D2226, p.22 (top): 0146, (bottom): HU63796, p.23 (top): HU63797, (bottom): HU63818, p.24 (left): HU63774, (centre): PS0019, (right): PST0696, p.25 (top): PST0770, (bottom): D8956, p.26 (left): HU36205, (bottom): HU36209, p.27 (top): HU36211, (bottom): TR2135, p.28 (top): HU69052, (bottom): 0710, p.29 (top): HU36210, (bottom): HU63828.

Image on p.12 (top) courtesy of Robert Opie.
Images on p.20 (top and centre) taken from posters *Useful Jobs that Girls Can Do* and *Simple Jobs that Boys Can Do,* and the advertisement on p.27 (bottom) reproduced with the permission of the Controller HMSO (Crown copyright).
Image on p.21 (top) courtesy of John Frost Newspapers.

Sources of quoted material:
Page 7:   Both taken from *The War Papers*, no.15, Peter Way and Marshall Cavendish Partworks Ltd., London, 1976
Page 10: Taken from Caroline Lang, *Keep Smiling Through: Women in the Second World War*, CUP, Cambridge, 1989, p.23
Page 13: Recipe taken from leaflet *Your Children's Food in Wartime*, issued by the Ministry of Food. Reproduced with permission of the Controller, HMSO (Crown copyright)
Page 14: Personal interview with author
Page 19: Taken from Michael Bentinck, ed., *War Time Women*, Michael Bentinck, 1998, p.88
Page 20: Personal interview with author
Page 22: Taken from Michael Bentinck, ed., *War Time Women*, Michael Bentinck, 1998, p.72
Page 23: Taken from Oonagh Hyndman, ed., *Wartime Kent*, Meresborough Books, Rainham, 1990, p.73
Page 26: Taken from *The War Papers*, no.35, Peter Way and Marshall Cavendish Partworks Ltd., London, 1976
Page 29: May Lawton quote taken from Mavis Nicholson, ed., *What Did You Do in the War, Mummy?*, Chatto and Windus, London, 1995, p.164
Page 29: Final quote taken from film commentary cited in Caroline Lang, *Keep Smiling Through: Women in the Second World War*, CUP, Cambridge, 1989, p.46

INDEX

Numbers in **bold** refer to pictures and captions.